Our

Stories

A Collection of Writings

Volume 6

Redlands Adult

Literacy Program

2023

Publication of this anthology is funded through
the generous support of the
Friends of A.K. Smiley Public Library

© 2023 Redlands Adult Literacy Program

Each author owns the copyright to his or her own work. This book may not be reproduced or distributed, in part or in whole, for profit. The views and opinions expressed in these writings are those of the authors and do not reflect the position or policies of the A.K. Smiley Public Library or any other funders of the Redlands Adult Literacy Program.

Cover Design by Renee Kennedy

Cover Photo by Peter Cruz

Back Cover Photos clockwise from top, right: Monday Morning Book Club by Diane Shimota. Cinderella Tran, Ponce-Suárez family, and Elen Alsabea by Yucaipa High School photography class taught by Redlands Adult Literacy volunteer Scott Kennedy.

Literacy Changes Lives!

Redlands Adult Literacy Program

The mission of the Redlands Adult Literacy Program is to provide professional and confidential tutoring in reading and writing to help learners in the Redlands community reach their literacy goals.

The Redlands Adult Literacy Program is funded by:

- The City of Redlands,
- A grant from California Library Literacy Services,
- Friends of A.K. Smiley Public Library,
- A.K. Smiley Public Library Endowment Fund, and
- Generous donations from service organizations and individuals who recognize the transformative power of literacy.

Acknowledgements

We express our sincerest gratitude to:

- adult learners who worked diligently to write and submit the entries in this anthology,
- volunteer tutors who supported their learners through the writing process,
- members of the Anthology Editorial Committee who provided a light edit of the learners' writing for spelling and understanding, but chose not to over-correct the writings in an effort to maintain the voice of each individual writer, and
- YMCA of the East Valley which provided meeting space for the Anthology Editorial Committee.

Anthology Editorial Committee Members:

Diane Adams, Francesca Astiazaran, Bonny Bowie, Darcel Cannady, Melany Chong, Michael DeWees, Katherine Gifford, Renee Kennedy, Diana Lamb, Glen Lastimosa, Maia Pawooskar, Sharon Regalado, Ann Sandin, Diane Shimota, Helene Shrader, Trudy Waldron, Jane Weldon, and Joan Wells.

Table of Contents

Message from the Library Director 7

Message from the Adult Literacy Coordinator 8

Message from the Anthology Editorial Committee 9

From the Heart 11

Home 27

My Story 45

Family and Friends 61

Closer to Nature 75

Unexpected Happenings 87

Reading Reflections 99

Family Literacy 109

Index of Authors 120

Our Services 124

Support Adult Literacy 127

"It is very hard to live in our world if you cannot read."

Raul Becerra, "Follow Your Dreams," p.47

"My mom did not know how to read and write. She sent us all to school."

Sotheavy Chev, "My Family Tree Memories," p.65

Message from the Library Director:

The A.K. Smiley Public Library Board of Trustees and I are very proud of the staff, tutors, and most importantly the learners who comprise our adult literacy program. *Literacy Changes Lives* is more than a slogan. One-to-one tutoring, small group book clubs, and writing workshops help our learners make progress on practical tasks such as filling out a job application and assisting with a child's homework, but also on the greater benefit of expanding the learner's ability to communicate with the world around them.

Six years ago our dedicated adult literacy coordinator, Diane Shimota had the inspired idea to assemble a compilation of written stories by our learners. Being able to share your individual thoughts, perspectives, and life experiences is a gift that many of us take for granted. Although writing can be both intimidating and difficult, the permanence of the written word has a special power to connect individuals, families, and communities. For some, the writing experience can be cathartic. As Maya Angelou said, "There is no greater agony than bearing an untold story inside you."

The learners who have contributed to this year's edition of Our Stories come from a variety of backgrounds. Some are longtime residents, others are more recent arrivals from other states or other countries. They have chosen to share with us their thoughts about their families, their life experiences, their hobbies, and their pets.

Congratulations to the learners for their achievement and thank you to the literacy staff and tutors who have helped them on their journey.

Don McCue, Director
A.K. Smiley Public Library

Message from the Adult Literacy Coordinator:

The Redlands Adult Literacy Program is proud to publish this sixth volume of the adult literacy anthology, Our Stories, A Collection of Writings. This volume includes the works of individual adult learners and a section of poetry and short writings from children of adult learners who participate in the family literacy program.

Adult learners, working with their tutors, create a vibrant learning community as they change their lives through literacy. We are honored, as a community, to hear the unique voices of the adult learners and to celebrate with them the gift of life-long learning.

In this volume, you will find writings *From the Heart* that express empathy and gratitude for those who have impacted the authors' lives; reflections about *Home*, wherever that may be; *My Story*, personal reflections and poems about the adult learners themselves; shared memories of *Family and Friends*; stories that take place outdoors, walking, hiking, or simply writing about being *Closer to Nature*. *Unexpected Happenings* are common to everyone, in this section, adult learners share some unplanned experiences. Finally, four authors wrote their *Reading Reflections* about books they read this year.

 As we publish this sixth volume of Our Stories, I reflect on the dedication of adult learners and their tutors, the many volunteers who support adult literacy, the community partners who offer space and support of adult literacy, and the donors who allow us to offer a free program which enables adults to reach their literacy goals. **Thank you for your ongoing support!** We look forward to continuing to work together on our community's journey to literacy.

Wishing everyone a very good read,

Diane Shimota, Adult Literacy Coordinator

Message from the Anthology Editorial Committee:

Our Stories is published annually by a dynamic adult learning community. Each volume reflects the efforts of many to whom we are grateful. Put simply, it takes a community to create an anthology. We are extremely fortunate to have so many learners, tutors, volunteers, library staff, and partners committed to learning and literacy within Redlands.

We are inspired by and grateful for the writings authors share with us each year. Learners and tutors work throughout the year to improve literacy skills and craft submissions for a regional *Writer-to-Writer Challenge* and for Our Stories. We encourage all, including emergent and beginning writers, to contribute to both writing opportunities. We all learn when journeys, stories, and ideas are shared.

Thank you to the members of the Anthology Editorial Committee who compiled and edited a volume that authentically represents our adult literacy community. We are grateful for the time and talent contributed by Redlands Adult Literacy Program staff members to enable this publication and for all they do to support adult learners and their families, tutors, and volunteers. Thank you also to the A.K. Smiley Public Library, its Board of Trustees, the Friends of A.K. Smiley Public Library, and all our donors and partners for helping us realize our vision and for sustaining the library's mission to serve as a center for lifelong learning for which "the only 'admission fee' is curiosity."

Joan Wells, Chair
Anthology Editorial Committee

From the Heart

"We have come to live in a multicultural country. Now you understand that we all do things in different ways, and every culture deserves to be honored and preserved."

Briseiry Roque, "Thank You!," p.16

My Tutor Helene
By Yanhong Zhou

I love Helene, she's my tutor. We know each other from the A.K. Smiley Library Literacy Program. We began working together in February 2019.

I was super nervous when I met her at the library. I carefully edited my English because I was worried that she wouldn't be able to understand me. I felt that talking with me was a kind of torture for her. But she listened patiently, never interrupting me and never saying: "I don't understand what you mean." When someone says this to me, it kills my confidence the most. I will suddenly feel that my brain is empty. She helps to correct my sentences, and she is good at using pictures and body language to help me understand accurately. Self-confidence is important in the process of learning a language. When I saw Helene could understand the sentences that I put together with my simple words, I felt more comfortable to talk more and more.

Besides self-confidence, persistence is also important. We tutored in the library every week. After a period of time I realized my English was improving, even though I still got a headache when I thought about having to go to the library the next week. Sometimes I even thought of finding an excuse to cancel our tutoring session. But now I am beginning to feel more relaxed. I have gone from understanding only 10% of my classes to being able to understand almost 90%. It was Helene's positive attitude that kept me from giving up. She continued to urge me to study while she was recovering from some health issues in 2020. During the pandemic we still tutored by Zoom. Because of these things I was one of a few students who received an award for over 100 hours of work to improve literacy throughout the year.

Although she didn't work in education before, she is my best teacher. She likes to read books. She has a lot of knowledge about the world, she seems to know everything! When I ask her a question, she can clearly explain the answer quickly. That is not something everyone can do. For example, once my husband took 10 minutes to explain something but I still didn't understand, it took Helene only 2 sentences to make the answer clear to me.

It's not just us, our two families have gotten to know each other also. Helene often discusses some of the content of my studies with her daughter at home, making me feel like I am one of her family members. When she sees examples of Asian hate, she tells me that she cares about my safety, which makes me feel so warm. In my family she is someone I often talk about. My husband says: "I feel you love Helene more than me." Yes, I do love her. She is intelligent, kind, positive and optimistic. She has taught me a lot, not only about English, but also life in general. One time we went to the Redlands Sunday market together. She told me that we must buy something because we need to support our city, otherwise, everyone will not have the enthusiasm to serve and contribute to community life. When I talked about the high crime rate among Black people, she said people of ALL colors do bad things.

I love Helene, she's my best friend. I have a dream: I want to visit Singapore with her. I want to be her guide and show her the beautiful country and share the delicious foods together. I will be her legs and she will be my mouth.

Tutor – Helene Shrader

The Good Samaritan
By Mina Ryan

This is a story from about thirty years ago. It touched my heart.

I had a flat tire on the freeway at 10 and Tennessee. I left my car, took my son who was two years old, and we walked to Coco's. I used the public pay phone to call my husband and my neighbor for help.

A man was waiting for us outside and offered to help to change the tire on my car. I asked him, "How did you know?" He said, "I followed you because I wanted to help you." I said, "Thank you, but that is okay. I have just called my husband and he is coming soon to fix the car. My neighbor is coming to pick me up because I have to pick up my other children from school."

I turned around and, to my surprise, the man had already started to change my tire. I went to talk to him and I asked him why he wanted to help me. I offered him some money and he would not take it. Again, I asked him why he wanted to help me.

Finally, he said, "I have a daughter and someday when she needs help, somebody will help her."

So, I remember that my mother always helped people and said the same thing. "Maybe someday, if you need help, someone will help you."

Now that I am a mother, I think the same way. I help when I can, so that someday somebody will help my children.

If you do good things, good things will happen to you. I believe in that.

Tutor – Pia Kennedy

My Daughter

By Cindy Yanke

My daughter...

My world...

My life...

My sunshine...

When I am with you, I am happy.

When I hear your voice, you bring comfort.

My daughter – you're my happiness.

When I hug you, I am loving you.

I give thanks to God that you sent a daughter to my life.

My only one – a beautiful daughter.

When you are smiling, my heart is fuller with joy.

When I hold your hands, you pull me to a secure and safe place.

When I am walking with you, you are the sunshine on the road.

When I stand alone, you talk to me and you sing for me.

When I cry, you hug me and you say you love me.

My daughter, you stand beside me.

You guide me to a bright, shining and never-never-ending peaceland.

Because of you, I am living in paradise.

Tutor – Martha Kennedy

Thank You!
By Briseiry Roque

I am Briseiry Roque. I moved here three years ago with my husband and my two children. The change has been a challenge for everyone, but I think it has been bigger for the two little ones. So, I want to tell you two, "Thanks." Although the decision to come here was not yours and is complex to understand, as we have told you, "We are looking for a better life." You have made a big effort every day to adapt to living here.

Thank you for being patient on our migratory journeys each year. Thank you for understanding that we wouldn't be able to bring all our belongings and bring just a few of your favorite toys. I know it was hard to say goodbye to our place, our friends and our family.

Thanks for being brave, attending a new school without knowing anyone, without having friends, and without being able to communicate. I remember, at first you felt discouraged when you did not reach the level of your class because you could not understand what the teacher was saying. Now you are very proud to show me your grades, you have done it!

I appreciate and celebrate the positive attitude you have had towards the changes that have occurred in our lives. I admire your ability to focus on good things that were happening around you, seeing you make your best effort every day has been an encouragement!

Also, you have new friends. Thanks for showing them respect and tolerance. We have come to live in a multicultural country. Now you understand that we all do things in different ways, and every culture deserves to be honored and preserved.

Thank you for conserving our culture, for participating proudly in our traditions and for continuing to enjoy the meals that our grandparents used to prepare. I am happy to see you enjoy new traditions and fun celebrations, too.

Thank you for taking every opportunity to learn something new. We can also celebrate that you are bilingual because you can speak English and Spanish very well.

Thanks for being my personal translator, you are faster and more reliable than Google. I appreciate you teaching me how to pronounce some words. "Nocturnal" is a big one. You should know that I enjoy that we are learning together. It makes me happy that you enjoy when I read you stories in Spanish, it is a way of sharing our oral tradition. I consider our language beautiful, and I am proud of your extensive vocabulary and fluency in Spanish.

Thank you for still building family bonds with your grandparents, aunts, uncles, cousins, and friends, because despite the distance you are sharing your life through calls and messages. The support of family and old friends has been essential to keeping us here. Their words of advice have been very helpful.

Thanks for trusting me with your aspirations, doubts, and fears. Thank you for believing me when I say, "Everything will be okay." I am grateful because everything that seemed like a challenge, you have turned into a strength.

Love, Mom... and I think Dad agrees.

Tutor – Darcel Cannady

Mom
By E. I.

MOM IS EVERYTHING

OUTSTANDING COOK

TOGETHER WE READ

HAPPY EVERYDAY

EASHA'S SUNSHINE

RADIANT AND LOVING

Letter to Mom
By E. I.

I love you because you are happy.

You are very special to me.

I love the food you make.

I love to read stories with you.

I love you mom,

♡ Love Easha

Letter from Mom
By J. I.

I love my Easha.

She is my life.

She is funny and naughty.

She is everything to me.

My shadow.

Lots of love,

J. I.

Tutor – Eileen Stephens

Fire That Changed My Life
By Apichat Sienglai

Last year on August 30, 2022, it was a difficult time for me because the house that I lived in burned. At about 6 p.m., I was working at my restaurant when my employer called me about the fire, and I felt panic and lost control of myself. It was my first experience like that in the U.S. After that, I still had to work until 8 p.m. I worried about many important things (passport, money, wallet) that I left in my room.

After work, my coworkers and I arrived at home where many firefighters were helping extinguish the fire. I felt very scared and worried. Then, officers allowed me to go inside with my co-worker to get the things in my room, which was a lot more damaged than the others. It was really dark so I used the light from my phone. We had to work quickly and spent about one hour. Finally, I luckily found all of my valuable things. However, all my stuff was wet. The Red Cross gave me about $200 for my damages. On that day, my employer brought me to her home. I had to dry everything in the garage, and I washed all my clothes. I slept for just a few hours, and after that I worked again the next day. I still felt lucky because I got all the valuable and important things but I lost some of my clothes and luggage.

A few days later, my employer said I couldn't stay at her house because she had a renter moving in. Suddenly, I felt upset. My manager tried to find a co-worker's house where I could stay. She found one, but it was far from my restaurant and I didn't have a car. I asked a co-worker named Ae to help me find a place close by. She called her mom. We went to her mom's house and talked about my story. We cried and asked her mom to let me stay. I had to wait until the next day for them to decide. In my opinion they had a difficult time deciding because they didn't know me. I hoped that Ae would vouch for me.

I am very thankful to Ae for helping me and introducing me to Claudia and Arlen. They called her and said I could stay. I moved in the next day. I felt happy. Mom and Dad have been kind and empathize with me a lot. They charge me just $100 per month. Mom's house is sweet and warm. I love Mom's house because it is really clean, beautiful and full of fresh air. It seemed that I got a new life.

When I first moved in, my English skills were very poor. Sometimes I would lose confidence when I spoke English with native speakers. My mom helped me contact Diane, a coordinator at the library. She made an appointment to test my English skills. My mom and I went to the YMCA to study English conversation together for the first time. I saw a lot of international students from Japan, Indonesia, Mexico, Spain and Egypt. I was so anxious because I didn't understand when my classmates spoke with me. However, I tried to overcome the situation. On my day off, I would walk from my mom's house to the YMCA for a conversation class. I knew that I had to spend a lot of time practicing my English skills. My mom really supported me.

After two weeks, my mom told me that I got a private English tutor. I felt excited again and hoped my English would improve. My tutor's name is Julia. She helps me a lot, and I am so proud of her. I learned a lot of technical methods from her. Furthermore, I feel more self-confidence and less stress speaking English with others. Confidence is a muscle. If there is more self-love, there is more self-confidence. I fortunately met my lovely and great mom and dad who help me. Everything is better because they are compassionate, inspiring and kind to me. I found many ways to improve my English such as watching YouTube and reading books. Every day, I have a growth mindset and my life is happier and more joyful. I am thankful for everyone who supports and helps me.

Tutor – Julia Naman

Dylan Rescued a Dog
By Ninon Sauceda

Dylan rescued a dog from the street. Dylan is one of my grandchildren. He started college this year and he works part time. He has a kind heart, and he is a very intelligent and handsome boy. One morning he called me and asked me if he could come over to my house. I said yes. Ten minutes later, Dylan arrived at my house with a dog. The dog was a sweet puppy, with white and black spots on her fur. The puppy ran away and went to my front yard. We all enjoyed seeing her running and playing. Dylan waited a few minutes, and he asked my husband and me if we wanted to keep her. We didn't say yes, but we told him, we can help you to find a new home for the puppy. Dylan was committed to finding a good home for the dog that he rescued.

After an hour Dylan said that his mom didn't want to keep the dog, because they already had two dogs. He didn't want to take the dog to the animal shelter. I told Dylan to wait, and I would go to ask a few neighbors if they wanted the dog. I also sent pictures of the dog to some friends and asked them if they wanted the puppy. Another hour passed and we couldn't find a new home for the dog. Dylan felt sad, he said, "Don't worry Grandma." I assured him that I would pray for the puppy not to end up in an animal shelter. When Dylan left, I felt sad too, because for the first time I couldn't help him.

During that week, I wondered every day if Dylan already found a home for the dog. I called him, and he said, "Mom is helping me. She put an ad on Facebook, and we're still waiting for somebody to respond."

The next day Dylan called me and told me that a married couple came and took the dog. They fell in love with the dog. It was a very nice moment when the dog saw them and right away ran towards them. There was a connection. They took the dog and Dylan felt very happy. My daughter and Dylan received an email from the couple a few days later. They named the puppy Bindi and sent pictures of her and her new home. Finally, Bindi was happy and Dylan too, because he found a good home for the dog.

The next day I went to my daughter's home. I saw Dylan, and I told him, "Grandpa and I are very happy that Bindi has a nice home. This is an example of your determination and good desire in your heart to find a good home for Bindi. You were persistent in not taking her to an animal shelter. Always remember you can reach all your goals in your life if you focus, and you put in the effort. You never give up, no matter what obstacle you confront. Your determination helped the dog to have a nice home."

Tutor - Corina Lopez

Mom
By Serena Oake

Is loving, strong, sure of herself

Knows a lot and is honest

Always Smiles

Taught me how to be positive and think for myself and be a force for good

Helped me sort out my problems

Showed me that I can be smart and strong

Special to me because of her love for me

Tutor – Ruth Christison

My Trials of Learning English
By Norma Acevedo

I was babysitting for a family of two kids, an 8-year-old boy and a 9-year-old girl. The girl would let me know that her brother was cursing at me but I couldn't pay attention to what the boy was saying to me, because I didn't know English. Because of that, I wasn't able to warn him properly, so he continued to curse at me. I was disappointed at the lack of my knowledge of the English language, and I thought to myself that I needed to learn English.

The first trial of learning English was 6 years later, when I enrolled in an ESL class, when I was 23 or 24 years old at the time. The class was disappointing because the students were talking about Spanish TV shows during class and still spoke in Spanish. I dropped out of the class, and I went back to work.

The second trial was in 2008, when the economy was bad, and I was unable to work because I was pregnant and I was suffering from pregnancy symptoms. I decided to go back to English classes for adults if my pregnancy symptoms would permit me to do so. When our child turned 3, we decided to move to Yuma, Arizona to start from zero again.

When our son turned 4, I decided to work at McDonald's and I worked there for 3 years overall. Even though my English wasn't good, I enrolled in a math class for one year. Later then, we moved to Redlands because of my husband's job.

One day during a meeting for my son, one of the moms told us about the Adult Literacy Program. When that happened, it was an important event that happened to me in my life. The literacy program and working with tutors has given me opportunities to gain more confidence to speak and think in English. It helps me in my daily life. Thank you all for this golden opportunity.

Tutor – Lois Van Cleve

Home

"I have learned that no matter where you call home, the key is to enjoy learning..."

Mila Gutierrez, "Life in Two Countries," p.29

Life in Two Countries
By Mila Gutierrez

This is a story of my two homes. I love Mexico and I love America. I can explain why it is important for me to share my journey between Mexico and America.

I was born in a beautiful small town in Mexico, but when I was 3 years old, my whole family moved to Mexico City. Adapting to a big city was interesting. Growing up was a good experience, seeing a lot of people everywhere, riding a subway or the bus, or even walking. Almost every day while I was in school, I visited different parks, restaurants, and flea markets. Mexico is a very social country and I had many friends. I had the privilege of living in Mexico for a short period of time. I had a wonderful experience growing up there and I always felt very independent at a young age.

I never imagined that my life would change by moving to another country. At first, I was in shock. I was going to leave everything that I knew behind: friends, school, and a very independent lifestyle. But I had no choice because I was too young to stay by myself. I became sick just thinking of moving to another country. My mom took me to the doctor and he prescribed vitamins. After I got better, my mom and two brothers and I flew to California. It was a big change from one country to another and I wondered how I was going to adapt to this new life.

I started high school right away, but there was a language problem. I did not know how to communicate with everyone. Completing my homework was difficult and I worried about having to take tests. I did not know how I was going to manage. It was very difficult. I knew for sure that I needed to be strong. After two years, I graduated from high school. The graduation ceremony was beautiful. I felt very important. "Yeah, I did it!" After the ceremony, all the graduates boarded a bus to Disneyland for Grad Night. Even though I did not officially become a U.S. citizen for a few more years, this experience made me feel no different than the American people I had come to know.

I feel that everyone I have encountered has treated me with respect and I appreciate that they have made me feel welcome in my second home. I have learned that no matter where you call home, the key is to enjoy learning, and to love and respect each other, and most important of all, that everything is going to be okay. Todo va ha estar bien.

Tutor – Frank Allen

My New Home
By Kwanlar Nyirady

My new chapter, new country, new weather and me. My name is Kwanlar Nyirady (Aem). I come from a small village in Thailand. When I first arrived here, I was shocked. I felt like a fish out of water. Everywhere I look is writing in English, and everyone speaks English. Where I grew up we spoke in Thai and we wrote Thai. I knew if I had to live here, I need to change fast. If I need to get around I need to be able to read. I began to search for the place that can help me. I find the beautiful library. They say they can help me for my English. I am learning to read and speak, and now I have become an American citizen. I am more confident in myself. I don't have to look down anymore. Now I can look up and be happy. I can read. Yes, I can read books. I love it. It is like I was blind and now I can see.

I love my new home. New seasons have come. Hot, cold, life gives us many flavors. Salty, sweet, bitter and it is all good. We have to find things to give us joy. We have to celebrate life as much as we can. Look up and smile. Life gives us so much joy to be happy. Look around you. You have everything, family, friends. Life is beautiful.

Tutor – Sue Fawcett

The Trinity Church
By Mark Corrin

In 2002, I started going to Sunday school at Trinity Church. Soon after I joined, I auditioned for the worship team at church. We sing songs like How Great is Our God in front of the congregation.

I recently started to lead the worshiping team at the church. I learned that God gave me a gift of music. I started leading the worshiping team and celebrating the Lord. Church is a wonderful thing!

I have many friends in my family of the Lord at church. I have been part of the church for 20 years. I am a worship leader for Sunday school class on Sundays. It makes me happy by singing and being part of the church.

Tutor – Martha Ganet

Light at the End of the Tunnel?
By Alexandra Suárez

Some people say, "There is a light at the end of the tunnel." I'm starting to understand what this idiom means in my daily life.

It's been almost two years now since I moved to the United States from Ecuador. I've had good days and very bad days. Those were the days when I asked myself, "What am I doing here? Why did I move from my beautiful country and away from everything I knew?"

I saw sadness and frustration in my little one's eyes. I saw my family struggle in many ways, as we tried to be part of this community. It was hard to understand the reactions towards us when we tried reaching out with kindness.

I am beginning to see God's grace again in our daily lives. It seems like everything is moving towards better days. I'm starting to see this country and Redlands as home.

So many positive things are happening. My husband recently received a raise. My daughter leaves school with a genuine smile. My 5-year-old son is bilingual! We bought a house with a pool, which I believe is a "must have" in order to survive the Redlands summers.

For myself, I'm now involved in the community! I'm part of our Adult Literacy and Family Literacy programs. I belong to a wonderful Moms Club. Most recently I started volunteering in my daughter's classroom. I was invited by my daughter's school to attend a Multilingual Conference for parents and teachers in Long Beach.

What I've learned from my new involvement is that I can't assume how things "should be" just because it is different from what I was used to. No more comparing cultures, we are all different and that's okay. I've put aside my fears and I'm now letting people get to know the real me. It brings me so much joy to see that my own experiences, good and bad, seem to be gifts to others. I plan to continue helping more people like me.

My family and I do see a "light at the end of the tunnel" now, and are filled with hope in our future here in beautiful Redlands.

Tutor – Barbara Vester

Going Back To My Country After 11 Years
Paola Munoz

It was not what I expected!

My biggest dream was one day to come back to my hometown and bring my kids to show them where I grew up.

Finally after 11 years, I had the opportunity to go back, but things were very different than I thought. I was in the process of legalizing myself in this country. After waiting a long time, I received an email from immigration with the date of my interview in Cd. Juarez, Chihuahua, Mexico. I was so excited. A lot of emotions came to me. I felt so happy and blessed but at the same time nervous and scared.

We got there four days before because I had a couple of appointments before the BIG DAY. The day arrived! On the day, I woke up feeling so nervous I could not eat anything! I had my interview at 11:30 am. I entered into the offices looking at everyone in the long line thinking every person had a different situation but everyone was hoping to go back home with our families.

The wait was over! I walked over to the officer who called my name. I remember his strong and scary gaze at me. We had a long interview. He was asking me a lot of questions and details, such as, how I entered into the USA and more about my marriage. I tried to relax and to answer all his questions. The officer was trying to confuse me with my own answers. After a long conversation the officer gave me a blue paper. He didn't say anything else, just "Have a good day." I grabbed all my documents and I walked out where my husband was waiting for me. He looked at me and with a huge smile on his face. He asked me, "Ready to go home?" I was so confused, I told him, "I don't know if I can go back home." The officer didn't tell me anything. He just gave me this paper. We read it but we didn't understand it! So we called the lawyer. After he saw the paper, he told us that we had to look for another sponsor in order to be able to come back to the country. My father-in-law was my sponsor. He was helping me but also he had sponsored eight people before me and his income could no longer sponsor one more person. The lawyer never asked him if he was helping somebody in the past.

After that long day, we went to our hotel to rest. We needed to think better because that situation changed all the plans we had. Before leaving the United States, I promised that whatever happened after the interview, we would visit the Basilica de Guadalupe in Mexico City to thank God and the Virgen de Guadalupe for everything. I had to stay in Mexico until my process was completed. My husband had to return home to take care of our three children. My youngest was only three years old. They needed me and I needed them!

My husband and our kids came to visit me every single weekend. It was very hard for him because he had to work the whole week, taking care of the kids and driving all way to Tijuana just to see me. It was a huge sacrifice for everyone!

Sponsoring is a huge responsibility. Finally my husband's uncle was able to help us. It took me six weeks to complete that process. That felt like an eternity!

When I received the passport, I didn't say anything to my husband. I went to the border for a short interview to get the stamp to enter legally into the country. I FaceTimed him from the border. I showed him my passport, he was very excited and surprised! It was around 9:00 pm Tuesday and he told me he could not be there until Saturday but he showed up the next day.

After all my struggles, I was home! I want to thank God for allowing me to return home with my family because not everyone can have that blessing!

Tutor – Karen Sharkey

My Life on a Ranch
By Salma R. Marquez

I have lived 25 years in this country after moving here from Mexico as a bride of 15 days married. I moved here because my husband got a job as a manager on a horse ranch. I had never lived on a ranch, although my father owned a ranch in Mexico.

For me it has been difficult, because I had to feed animals, clean stalls, give medicine, while taking care of my family. We raised a son and a daughter on this ranch.

I have to learn to like and value tranquility that is living here. I would not change anything about living on a ranch.

At the moment, I am learning how to make different types of cheeses, and this can be very difficult, but I am slowly understanding the process.

Every morning I wake up to find eggs. Sometimes it is tiring because there are too many chickens. Although it is a lot of work, I enjoy it because I love animals.

Tutor – Nancy K. Rogers

School in Punjab
By K.K.

When I started elementary school in Punjab, I would have to walk half a mile to get there. I had classes every Monday to Saturday and only Sundays off. During the summers we would get only one month off of school, and we still had a lot of homework to do during the break. All of my subjects were taught in Punjabi, and I only started to learn English when I moved up to the sixth grade, when I also learned to read and write in Hindi.

During school we would sit on mats, because there were no desks or chairs for us to use. Oftentimes we would go sit outside under the shade of the trees for our classes. Also, we had no paper to use, so every student would use a wooden board that would be covered in clay. When the board was full of writing, we would wash off the black ink and add more clay to the board and let it dry in the sun to use again.

Now, schools in Punjab are a lot different from when I was in school, and very similar to the schools here. There are busses to take children to and from school, they have plenty of school supplies to use, and English is taught a lot earlier. Overall, I'm grateful for my experiences, but I'm glad that there are more resources for children in Punjab now.

Tutor – Corinne Scatliffe

When I Was Growing Up
By C. Pineda

Part of my life in a short story: As I can recall, my parents used to move from place to place. I hardly remember when we were moving from far away to San Francisco in Durango, Mexico. So my father was carrying me inside of a grain sack. I was very little, probably very tired of walking too. This trip is always in my mind and I liked it very much because after that trip, I kept playing with the grain sack. One of my fingers got stuck inside one of the holes of the sack until my finger was bluish.

On another occasion, my parents were moving again, but this time they wanted to leave me and my little sister with my older sister. It didn't work the way they planned because when I saw that they were leaving me, I started crying as hard as I could. My crying convinced my father, and he told my older sister to let me go. We walked all day and part of the night. When we arrived at our destination, my younger sister and I were inside of the sacks, one on each side on top of a horse. We slept most of the time. That place was very cold. The most funny thing that I remember when we were living in this place was when we were warming ourselves on the chimney. When I got down from the chimney, since the floor was wet and slippery, I slid right on my back. My younger sister made fun of me laughing, "Haha that's what you get for being stupid." Not even five minutes passed, when she got down and she fell right on her back. But this time wasn't funny anymore, this time she was crying like someone was kidnapping her.

One of the scary moments that I remember happened when my sister and I were staying with my grandma almost in the middle of the forest. Grandma went to look for the goats, but she took too long so my sister and I thought that she wasn't going to be back.

We decided to pack and leave the house, in the direction of my mother's house. We had already left when my grandma got home, so she couldn't find us and went to look for us. But because we were so little, we got lost on the way to our mother's house. By the time we were almost arriving, my grandma had already gone to our mother's house, didn't see us there, and was heading back to her house. Right before she came out of the ranch and was heading to her house, she found us. Then she took us to my mother, just to let her know that she did find us, and we went back with her. On the way back, the night fell on us. We couldn't see the way, so we slept by a stream with one of the dogs by our heads and another by our feet. In the morning, we started the way home. When my father found out what happened, he was very worried. He started to tell us that we were very lucky that God took care of us, because in that particular place lived a variety of animals, like mountain lions and so on.

Soon enough, my brother took the dogs for a hunt. On the way back home, a lion attacked them. He shouted at the lion but he didn't kill it, so the lion ran straight to my brother. My brother hit the lion with the back of his rifle and broke the back of it. Luckily my brother came home safe. When I saw him, his face was pale. He was telling us that when the lion was already on the ground, the dogs tried to bite it. With a single kick, the lion threw the dogs very far away.

In conclusion, I want to thank my Creator for putting these two people in my life: Diane from the Literacy Program and Nancy, my tutor. Because without them, this story would not be possible. God bless them and to all of you who read my story.

Tutor – Nancy Luong

Singing

By Ma, Isabel Vidrio

Singing at the market was one of the most exciting experiences of my life.

Mom sent my sister Gloria and me to the food store to buy cinnamon. It was nighttime. My uncles asked me to sing because they knew I liked singing. I asked them, "What do you want me to sing?" I only knew three songs. I sang "La Copa Vacia" for them, and they gave me some coins. I bought a package of cookies with the money.

When we got back, we were eating the cookies and my sister asked me for more. I told her to, "Sing!" She got angry with me because she was embarrassed to sing.

My memory of getting coins to buy cookies is so funny and exciting to me.

Tutor – Jeanne Fortier

Burritos with Salt
By Yesenia JV

When I was a child, my mother made tortillas and when the tortilla was ready it was soft. She would squish it to make burritos with salt. A few years ago, when my children were 6 and 3 years old, I would sometimes also make tortillas. I remembered the burritos that my mother made for me. I made burritos for my children and I offered them. My oldest son tells me, "What is this?" I told him, "A burrito, try it. My mom used to make them for me when I was little." He told me, "I don't like it. I don't want to eat that." I was surprised that he didn't want to eat that because when I was a child, I really liked it.

Tutor – Joan Prehoda

Wisconsin
By Cindy Yanke

Wisconsin is a beautiful state. I have many memories from my time living there. My husband and I and my son, and my daughter used to live in Madison, Wisconsin, the capital city. My house was close to a lake. Our house was a two-story house. In front of the house, we had a patio and a swing and some chairs.

Summertime we sat on a swing drinking a soda. We sang. We laughed with my husband and two children. We were enjoying a summer day. Some days our family would take a fishing pole, and we walk to the lake about two blocks from home. We got there and we look for a place to sit close to the water, and we start to put the fishing pole line in the water, catching fish. We were catching lots of fish. We put the fish in the bucket. Then we brought the fish home, and some of the fish I cooked for my family. We all enjoyed eating fish. I imagine I am there today.

This is what I see:

When summer is slowly going away, fall is coming. Under the Wisconsin blue sky, fall arrives. The mountains and fields and all the trees' leaves change to red, yellow, brown, orange, purple, and turn to many colors. It is just like a beautiful painting, a picture. Many small towns and farmland fields are covered with grown vegetables, and yellow corn fields for miles.

Also, many cows are on the field eating the grass. Some are baby cows with mama, and they are running, and they have fun beside the mama. Farmers raise lots of cows for milk. They use milk to make butter and cheese.

When you stop at the little village or town store, you see Wisconsin cheese. They are fresh and yummy. Also, Wisconsin people are very friendly and invite you to their house for coffee or cookies. When you are driving on the road looking at each side of the field, you can see many kinds of trees and some branches with many colored leaves and flowers. When the wind blows away, you can smell the flower fragrance. I feel fresh and wonderful.

I keep on driving past farmland and trees. Sometimes you see a deer on the road or bushes. Many of them are big and small deer. No matter where you drive, where you go, the sky is blue; the air is fresh, and people are friendly. The view is beautiful with lots of trees – country roads, everywhere. Wisconsin has lots of farmland and cows, deer, and sweet corn and cheese. Also, Wisconsin milk is rich and fresh – so good! I never stop thinking about Wisconsin, and my heart is always with Wisconsin.

Tutor – Martha Kennedy

My Story

"I told myself that I did my best.
Hard times come and go.
Now I'm ready to tackle another day."

Sotheavy Chev, "I Did My Best," p. 50

Follow Your Dreams
By Raul Becerra

I am not a quitter. I will find ways to get the answers. I like hiking and camping with my family. I like being outdoors and seeing the sunrise.

I am a hard worker.

I like to play cards with my mom and dad. I am a happy person and I like to cook. I am a grandfather of a two-year-old granddaughter. I want to improve my reading and writing skills. I am nervous when I have to read in public. It is very hard to live in our world if you cannot read. My dream is to improve my reading skills.

Tutor – Susan Hodges

Peter Cruz and his tutor, Donita Remington, on the front steps of A.K. Smiley Public Library. This photograph and the front cover photo were taken by Peter Cruz in July 2023.

My Love for Photography
By Peter Cruz

I have been interested in photography ever since high school. I saw my brother taking a photography class and that got my interest when I saw how much he enjoyed it.

When I started my first year of college, I saw a group of people taking photos around campus. I later saw the photos in a newspaper I picked up. I decided to take a photography class and I have been taking photos ever since.

My favorite type of photography is portrait and family photos, my family has always kept me taking photos at parties and events.

Recently I saw a photo booth at a family event. It piqued my interest so I decided to try a photo booth myself, but in my own way. I enjoyed it a lot, so I decided to take photos for my sister's baby shower. Everyone was amazed at the work I did. My little nephew enjoyed it so much that he was helping me get people involved in taking photos. He laughed and said he was going to take my job. I was so happy how it impacted him.

I also recently did a favor for my uncle restoring my grandmother's photo that was about 50 years old. He was very excited and happy with how the photo came out.

Photography is important to me because of the way people get a chance to enjoy each other's company. I like to be able to gather a person's ideas of how they want their photos to look, and then add my creativity to make the photo come to life. I enjoy taking photos because it connects people in different creative events.

I feel the ability to do something you enjoy as a career is so important. It makes me so happy to see the expression on a person's face as they enjoy something that I helped create. I would never have had the ability to create new friendships or record special moments, if it were not for the love I have for photography.

Tutor – Donita Remington

I Did My Best
By Sotheavy Chev

Being a wife and a mom is a lot. Being a great wife and best mom is hard. I don't worry much about how I am going to meet the expectations of others. I worry more about meeting my own expectations. I always want to be the best at everything I do.

The day I felt that I was not good enough, it made me want to run away. But, then I said my prayers, read my scripture, and talked with best friends. Writing down all my problems, going for a walk, and listening to uplifting music helped me calm down. I told myself that I did my best. Hard times come and go. Now I'm ready to tackle another day.

Tutor – Joan Wells

My Life
By Alec B.

Alec

Bendy, Twisty, Creative, Smart

Drinks Pepsi

Loves games

Listens to music

Good at making friends

Good at fixing my own problems

I dance to forget

Tutor – Kathleen VanderWal

My Tutoring Story
By Frank Allen, Tutor

My tutoring journey started in the early 1990s during a period of unemployment. My church in Garden Grove had begun a pilot program offering classes in ESL (English as a Second Language) to Hispanic residents in our community. To occupy my time, I volunteered to become a tutor. The director of the program recognized that I had a unique ability to engage with and relate to the students because I was foreign-born myself. I was born in Indonesia and raised and educated in the Netherlands. In high school I learned to become fluent in English, French, and German in addition to my native Dutch language. She encouraged me to contact the Laubach Literacy Program of Orange County. This organization was dedicated to tutoring basic adult literacy skills. I attended several training classes with this organization and earned several certificates for working with literacy-challenged adults.

The director of Laubach Literacy in Orange County encouraged me to investigate an opportunity with AmeriCorps, a national program to encourage participation in community service programs. The Santa Ana Public Library was seeking participants with AmeriCorps to launch an ESL program in their three library branches. I spent two years working full-time in Santa Ana's public library system, tutoring students in the Santa Ana School District with math, reading, and homework assistance. When my AmeriCorps obligation was complete, I received a grant to enroll in a degree completion program at a local college in Fullerton.

Over the years of my earlier employment experiences, I had taken enough community college courses and accumulated enough credits to transfer to a university. There was a school in Fullerton that had a program for working adults to complete a BS degree in

18 months. That year-and-a-half flew by very fast, and with my BS degree I was ready to pursue my California Teaching Credential for Adult Education.

I continued tutoring, but now as a credentialed instructor, I began teaching Adult ESL with the Santa Ana School District. This was quite a change from tutoring one-on-one and small groups. I was now teaching a class of up to 35 students. I really enjoyed seeing those students improve their language skills.

While still working in Orange County, my wife and I made the decision to move to the Riverside/Corona area, about halfway between Garden Grove and Yucaipa, to be nearer to my family. After our move to Riverside, the commute to Santa Ana was difficult, so I started teaching for the Corona-Norco School District and the Riverside Adult School.

I retired from teaching in 2010, but resumed tutoring a small group at my church in Corona.

In 2017 we moved to Calimesa to be closer to our daughter, who lives in Yucaipa with her family. Shortly after our move, I began tutoring for the Redlands library. Our own city library is very small and has no space for tutoring, so I started looking for other nearby libraries. In January of 2022, I began tutoring ESL for the Beaumont Library District.

The two libraries keep me pretty busy. My teaching years have helped me become a better tutor, I plan to continue as long as my health allows it.

My Diamante Poem
By Ma, Isabel Vidrio

Isabel

positive   brave

busy   active   works

mother   daughter   student   counselor

cooking   driving   helping

empathetic   kind

consultant

Tutor – Jeanne Fortier

Me Myself I
By Phillip Goff

Phillip

strong   hardworking

stacking   packing   replenishing

provider   babysitter   protector   kidder

paying   listening   cooking

polite patient

Goff

Tutor – Ann Sandin

Pepito Caballero Castañeda Roque
By Armando Castañeda

I'm going to tell you a story

About a marvelous being

That has been with me together

Leaving uncountable disasters

He is big and very small

He is chiseled and fat

His ideas are brilliant

But he is the dumbest

And here is a thing that I have accepted

Whatever he encounters now

He will face with courage in his soul

On his journeys, you can see

All the triumphs he collects

Without surrender

In the world he has traveled

Many friends and acquaintances

Have been scattered here and there

All their energy is with him now

And always will be

Making him stronger and all around better

A thousand problems he has solved

Many more he has created

But one thing you know for sure

All is coming from his soul

But let's go back a little, let me tell you a bit more about Pepito Caballero. He was born in 2015 and has been on many journeys since that time, but don't let this fact fool you. Pepito Caballero is a grown-up, well almost. I must confess he is also a crying baby who throws tantrums and needs a lot of love even when you don't notice.

But let's go to the point, you are here to listen to a history, and this is the story.

Ode

The story I will share is a tribute to something particular, the ode is a poem you must sing

It was created in Greece to transmit histories in times when reading and writing did not exist. This ode, in particular, is irregular, philosophical and heroic

Once upon a time in a land far away there was a knight that was very talented and famous but still had a lot of things to learn

While the knight was on one of his many quests, a beautiful damsel appeared around town and he fell in love with her, that's when everything turned upside down

A new life began with scores of doubts and worries

Many fears and frowns were coming

What if he isn't smart and handsome

What if he isn't kind and strong

With all these fears and challenges, the knight and maiden lived humbly between ghosts, savage cats, and ugly houses

But these difficult things also came with good people who made them strong

The salve was a new little knight that filled their hearts with love, he took away all the fears and that was when the knight discovered he didn't know as much as he thought

The mini knight had become the teacher, so smart and very sharp

Pepito was brave in his own way. He was a handsome little knight who would fill you up with light and love

One day the little knight fell silent because the big knight in the story got lost

During another day on the road to adventure, the big knight and the princess were driving with Pepito, when suddenly their car turned over on the road. Pepito was afraid, but everything was okay

Good friends came to help, and we moved on from the bad day. Then a week later, something happened that woke Pepito up

In the same spot that the car had turned over they saw two crosses. Pepito felt like a ghost, and we knew we had to be grateful for this life

And then the little princess arrived. Inside, she was already scratching mom's belly, a lovely tornado and, God, she was very stubborn

Next, came another challenge of traveling adrift, Pepito attended another school, got a new job, and left an old one to stay at home

All was new

Without friends and without speaking the language, they faced each other without reservations and triumphed

The message I leave you is that Pepito Caballero did not win because he was spectacular

The triumph came from the people who supported him, his children and his wife, the school teachers, the neighbors, the grandparents, and even the dog they saved

So here I say goodbye and I ask only one thing, that when you do something great you too must share all your good seeds so that they can grow up in another person's life

Tutor – Francesca Astiazaran

Family and Friends

"So, let's explore — communication, language, culture, traditions, celebrations and all the ways that we can honor one another."

Darcel Cannady & Briseiry Roque, "Our New Language," p. 72

Talking with my Grandfather
By Rebeca Dominguez

When I was little I loved to talk with my grandpa Enrique because he always had interesting things to share. My grandfather was a Yaqui Indian, his whole family lived in the Sierra of Sonora. He did not know how to write or read Spanish, but he was very good at doing math problems in his head without needing a paper and pencil. He knew a lot about healing herbs and plants. His mother and grandmother were the people who healed in his community. He never went to the doctor when he felt bad, he only cured himself. He knew what herbs he needed and went to the bush to look for them.

All the times he counted the moons, that was his calendar. He checked all the time, the sun, the stars, the weather, the moons, with that he knew if it was going to be a good day for fishing or planting. When a great aunt of my mother died, I remember very well her aunt told her, I want a plum and my grandfather told her to give it to her. It's the last thing she's going to eat, and when she finished it, she died and he said they are here for her and she left.

He had in his command a cooperative, that was a group of people who went fishing, and he delivered the product they caught to the packers, that was where he put his brain to work for math doing sums of tons and collecting the money to take it and pay to the fishermen. He was an amazing person, he died when he was 106 years old and he knew when it was just his time. He called my mom to spend the last couple of months with her, "It's about time, come to see me before I leave," and he left very happy with the whole family together.

Tutor – Frank Allen

The Birth of My First Child
By Yanetzy Pacheco

Twelve years ago, I was working at the university in Mexicali. I was 24 weeks pregnant and I started to feel contractions. I asked my friend about it, and she told me that maybe that's not normal. She told me that when I go home, I should rest on the bed with my legs up over a pillow. I started bleeding and my mom took me to the emergency room. The doctor said that the baby is coming and he can't do anything. He recommended I have my baby in the USA because he will have a higher chance of living than if he was born in Mexico. My aunts and I crossed the border to Calexico, California, and my baby was born premature at 24 weeks. The hospital didn't have the resources to keep my baby alive, so they decided to take him to San Diego in a helicopter. My baby stayed at the hospital for around 3 months. Now, thank God, my son is full of energy and healthy.

The Birth of My Second Child

My first son was 8 years old when I became pregnant again. I woke up one morning to take my son to school when I began to feel weird. My stomach was upset and I felt very nauseous. I felt like I did during my first pregnancy. That morning I went to the pharmacy to buy a pregnancy test. I felt very nervous about it. Of course, I would like to be pregnant, but at the same time I felt like I was not ready yet. When the test came out positive I felt confused but also happy at the same time. I waited until my husband's birthday to surprise him with the news. He was happy about it and that made me feel more happy and comfortable. I was in my 26th week, when I noticed that I was bleeding. My husband was too far away to help me. I called my aunt and she took me to the hospital. My 2nd baby was born premature. He stayed at the hospital for 3 months and then he was ready to go home. Now, at 5 years old, my son is a healthy, curious, and a happy boy.

Tutor – Natalie Herrera

My Family Tree Memories
By Sotheavy Chev

My name is Sotheavy. I was born in a small village in Cambodia. I grew up in a big family. I have three brothers and a sister. My house and all my cousins' houses were on the same street. It made me feel like I was in a big family. I made a lot of memories with my big, big family, but I got to know only one of each set of my grandparents personally. Two of my grandparents died before I was born.

My father's father died before I was born. I only heard his story from others. He was a driver for a royal palace. He could speak French, served in World War II helping France, and had many wives.

My grandmother on my father's side got married at a young age, 16 years old. She had 7 kids that lived. She became a widow and raised all her children all by herself. She was super strong, smart, had a lot of self-control, was expert on preparedness, calm, and hard working.

My mother's father was a gamer. He loved playing sports. I did not like him much because he drank a lot. He asked me to go to the store to get him alcohol every day. Whenever he came to visit us, he would work for my mom's farm. He counted days to see how much he would get paid.

My mother's mother, I did not know in person. She also died before I came into this world. She was a farmer as well. She worked hard each day. She had 5 kids.

My dad was a fisherman, an electrician, and a cow witch doctor. He helped my mom work on the farm once in a while. Farmers at that time worked with their hands and cows with no technology to help. My dad is super friendly and kind to others. He loves technology. We were the first family to have technology. He could fix anything. He only finished grade 12 in school.

My mom is a housewife. She is the hardest working farmer in the entire village. She has been through a lot. She loves to take care of others. She cooks a lot of food, loves parties. She is super patient, strong physically and mentally, and she has big dreams.

I grew up in a better generation, time, and place than all my grandparents and my parents did. My mom did not know how to read and write. She sent us all to school.

Tutor – Joan Wells

My Dogs
By Rossy Le

Today I want to tell the story of my three dogs: Luna, Mochi, and Tofu.

Luna is a Dalmatian, a beautiful dog. She came to our family when she was three months old. She is a happy, naughty, and loving dog. We didn't see anything strange in her. The days went by when we realized that she did not listen to us when we talked to her. She always tried to glue her body to us because she felt safe. She was afraid and we didn't understand why. We took her to the vet and they told us that she was deaf. Many Dalmatians have a genetic problem where they are born deaf. For my family, we changed everything, but a very great love grew to protect her and make her feel happy and safe. We started talking to her with signs that were easy for her to understand. Now she is five years old, happy, and the queen of the house.

Mochi is a beautiful black Sharpei, full of wrinkles all over her body. She came to us when she was two months old. She's a funny, naughty and very busy dog. She is always looking out the window and wanting to go out to the backyard to look for the smell of cats. She doesn't like cats. Sharpeis are very protective and take care of their space. They don't trust anyone. She is happy and makes Luna feel safe. Now Mochi is two years old.

Tofu arrived when he was three months old. The universe sent my husband to work on the streets of Pasadena. A man passed by with Bombon (a dog). That was the name when he first arrived at our house. The man asked my husband if he wanted a dog. He said he couldn't take care of it because he lived in an apartment. The dog had already lived in two other houses. My husband called me to see if we could look for a place. He said to me that he had to bring him because the dog's eyes asked for help. When he finished work, he was to pick up Bombon. He was so loving and he came to grab my husband's hand all the time. They fell in love. In a week, we found two houses. Neither one could take care of him. In less than two months, he was with five families. My husband said that he chose us and we were not going to let him suffer more; he would stay with us. It was a difficult decision because we already had Luna and Mochi. We adopted him with a lot of love and we changed his name to Tofu. We wanted him to forget his past.

We had a problem; Mochi didn't accept that there was a male dog that arrived at the house. She was sad and didn't eat for three days. It was very difficult for her to accept it. After a week and from then on, they were the best family. Tofu takes care of the girls and plays all day long. He controls the two sisters; he is the king of the house. He is a mixed terrier; we don't know what breed he is. He is one year and three months old.

Luna, Mochi, and Tofu came to be a part of our family. Now my husband and I have a 24-year-old daughter, Luna, Mochi, and Tofu. They are 4 children full of a lot of love.

Tutor – Sharon Regalado

Gratitude at Dawn
By Elen Alsabea

It was a stormy, cold, dark night filled with fear and sadness because of the war that was happening all around us in Syria.

We were sharing a space to sleep in a small, dark, cold room. No heat or electricity, just the fear from the bombs sounding all around.

I was so sad and pessimistic thinking that all the peaceful life that we had before was gone in one day. I thought I didn't have anything to make me hopeful for the future.

I opened my eyes and saw my husband and my little kids sleeping peacefully next to me. That moment opened the hopeful door from inside my heart. I have my lovely family. I have a lot to be grateful for.

Tutor – Trudy Waldron

A Wonderful Family
By Manuela Ballesteros

After we moved to Loma Linda in 2006, I started to work with a wonderful family, a doctor, his wife, and their son. They were very nice people, kind and generous. They had a dog and a cockatoo named Bella. They gave me the key of their house. I started to work once a week cleaning their house from 8:00am to 2:00pm.

They called me Nelly affectionately, I became very fond of them and they of me. The first task was to feed Bella and clean her cage. After a while of working for them, I was very surprised that Bella learned to say my name "Nelly." I was very happy. It was an honor for me to hear Bella say my name.

Every week I went to work, and when I opened the door of the doctor's house, Bella greeted me saying "Nelly" and repeated my name several times while I was working. That made me happy. I always talked to her while I was working, because the dog and Bella were my company during the six hours of work. When I finished working I said goodbye to Bella, and when I left I closed the door and locked it. Later when his wife returned to her house she would call me to say thank you. During the time that I worked, I worked very comfortably. It was very relaxing for me to listen to the classical music that the doctor and his wife had in every room throughout the day.

One day they gave me the news that they had to move to another state because the doctor was offered the position of General Director of the hospital there. I was very sad. I will always remember the doctor, his family, and Bella with love. It is a beautiful memory. I will never forget it.

Tutor – Patty Loo

Our New Language
By Darcel Cannady and Briseiry Roque

This year Bris and I have continued our learning journey. In our sessions we both realize that we talk a lot with our hands. We have discovered that it is another form of expression for us. So much so, that we can barely talk without an accompanying hand movement.

After one of our learning sessions, while exiting the library, we encountered two people using Sign Language. We both were instantly curious and set out on our Sign Language exploration.

Bris read on the internet that Sign Language is older than any written language. It was used especially with people of different languages because the phonetic utterances between languages were difficult for each culture to understand.

I actually enrolled in an American Sign Language (ASL) course at Crafton Hills College, while Bris found an online class in Mexican Sign Language (LSM), not <u>Spanish</u> Sign Language.

We quickly found out that there are as many ways to "sign" as there are languages. Signing can be based on language, region, and/or culture.

ASL is a basic for American English speakers. However, in a quirky nuance to that, my ASL instructor has a poster in her class that says, "English is NOT my first language."

Go figure? I think she means that signing has its own rules, that do not necessarily align with the rules of speaking the English language.

While sharing what we each have learned, Bris and I found many similarities and quite a few differences.

For example, in American Sign Language (ASL) "Yes" is (two knocks with a closed fist), while in Mexican Sign Language (LSM) "Yes" is (pinky finger bent down twice).

While "No" is pretty much the same (tap down twice with the first two fingers).

The good thing is that the basic alphabet is essentially the same, so we do have a common place to start with.

Hello   **ASL** (salute flat hand from forehead)

Hola   **LSM** (salute first two fingers crossed from the forehead)

Friend   **ASL** (interlocking index fingers – right crossing over to left and flip)

Amigo   **LSM** (right hand claps over left fist)

How are you   **ASL** (point towards yourself with both thumbs, all fingers folded in, rotate thumbs out, point to the person you are speaking to)

Como estas   **LSM** (both hands in "c" position, bring together, rotate and pull down with all fingers pointing inward in cuplike position)

Please   **ASL** (right flat hand make a circle at chest)

Por favor   **LSM** (place both palms together, move forward twice)

Thank you   **ASL** (right flat hand touch chin, flip out)

Gracias   **LSM** (tap bent middle finger into open flat left hand)

Last but not least is our favorite, in ASL

Favorite – (tap bent middle finger to chin twice)

Beans – (left extended index finger, right hand covers left finger and twists down twice)

Rice – ("R" sign in right hand; first two fingers crossed, scoop out of the left hand in a cup shape, bringing crossed fingers to lips)

So, let's explore – communication, language, culture, traditions, celebrations and all the ways that we can honor one another. It is our hope that we will discover that we are not so different, that we really are more alike.

Different ASL (cross index fingers, move apart)

Alike   ASL ("Y" sign, back and forth)

On a Sunny Day
By Mark Corrin

A friend is like a sunny day.

The sun feels nice.

I feel nice with my friends.

The Lord makes it sunny,

and the Lord loves

me and my friends.

Tutor – Martha Ganet

Closer to Nature

"I never imagined that I was going to experience a magical moment!"

Emma Velázquez, "My Wonderful Short Visit to La Paz, Baja California," p. 77

My Wonderful Short Visit to La Paz, Baja California
By Emma Velázquez

In 2016, a friend of mine invited me to go to La Paz to a celebration that was going to be held at the city theater. While I was there, I felt excited just by walking on the beach and going in and out of the tourist shops. It was a pleasure to eat fresh seafood and to enjoy seeing the sunset in the evening. I didn't think I could feel happier!

After a couple days, my friend and I decided to go whale watching in the bay. I didn't know anything about the whales or the place where we were going, so I was not expecting too much. We went to the boat station to buy the tickets to ride the small boat that took us further out in the ocean. The boat operator told us that the whales traveled from Antarctica. It takes them about three months to get to the bay where the water is warmer and they have their babies.

After about thirty minutes, we got there, so the operator stopped the small boat motor. And right away we could see all the big gray whales near the other boats that arrived earlier. We were told that if we wanted the whales to come to us, we needed to put our hands in the water and move them back and forth to make noise, so the whales could hear it and come over. Indeed, it happened just the way they said. That's when the excitement started.

A mama whale and her baby came to us. My friend and I started to say nice, positive words to both of them. The mama whale and her baby swam under and around our boat several times for about 15 to 20 minutes. We were saying things to them like "Good morning...How are you?...You are beautiful!...Wow your baby is big!...Are you happy?"

It was hard to believe that they were swimming so close to us. I felt very happy to be living in the moment. I could feel the mama whale and her baby's happiness. Then, the extra special moment came. While we kept saying nice words, all of the sudden the mom came out of the water and opened her big mouth. I got scared! She was in front of me! I stood still for a second, then I told myself, "I don't have to be scared. She came up to say good morning!" I got closer to touch her face. That was my magical moment!!

I never imagined that I was going to experience a magical moment! Whale watching turned out to be whale touching.

Tutor—Ann Sandin

Walking in the Hills
By Manuela Ballesteros

I like to walk in the hills. When I walk, I can meditate, and that gives me peace and at the same time I can enjoy the beautiful view of the city and my neighborhood from the top of the hills. I love to see all the wonders that God created like the sky, the clouds, the mountains, the snow, and the trees.

I like to walk early in the morning when the weather is clear at 5:30am or 6:00am, for an hour and a half or two hours. I love to see the new dawn, the sun when it just begins to rise behind the mountains. In spring, I enjoy seeing all kinds of wildflowers especially California poppies and goldfields. I also love seeing beautiful rainbows appearing in the sky after the rain.

In spring, I also like to smell the perfume of the flowers and orange blossoms. I enjoy feeling the air and breeze on my face, the rain, and the snow. And when it is raining and snowing, I like to taste the raindrops and the snowflakes melting in my mouth.

I love listening to the singing of the birds, the sound of fountains, and the murmur of streams. All this relaxes me and gives me peace and serenity. These are some of the things that give me pleasure when I go for a walk.

Tutor – Patty Loo

Hike to Hollywood Sign
By Apichat Sienglai

Many years ago, I was really sick and needed to change everything in my life. When I had a day off, I started to hike the Hollywood Mountain, which wasn't far from my house. The first time I tried, I could only hike about five minutes. I was tired but I saw that old people and children could hike. The next time I tried I still was exhausted, but I could hike further. I decided to hike every day, so I had to wake up early to have more time to practice hiking. It was difficult for me because some routes were more steep and were about five miles to the top, taking me about two hours. However, every day I gradually hiked step by step. If I was tired, I stopped hiking for a few minutes and drank water. After that, I tried to hike more if I could. It was important that I had self-discipline to hike every morning before I worked. I needed to see the beautiful and amazing views on the top of the mountain, which inspired me to build more confidence and energy. One day, I saw a handicapped man who could hike the mountain. I was very surprised and impressed and hoped that I could do the same as this man. I tried to hike higher and higher up the mountain. Every time I saw him, I said, "Hi," and I cried. He was my idol and hero. Sometimes I brought fruit and water when I was hiking. If I had time, I would take a lot of pictures of the beautiful flowers and plants. When I finally went to the highest point, I was so proud of myself because I could do it. The air was so fresh. Then I would meditate for about 20 minutes to calm myself to reduce stress and panic. When I hiked down I felt happy and joyful. In the summer season, the weather was very hot and I was afraid of heat stroke, yet it was so fantastic and mesmerizing. My body was drenched in sweat and sunburned. It made my muscles stronger and filled me with more energy.

Every day many tourists visit the famous Griffith Observatory, where they take beautiful pictures at sunset. There are many routes to hike to the top of the mountain with a variety of gorgeous nature paths. The mountain is massive. I loved to spend a lot of time there because it made me happy and I observed self-awareness and self-love. I knew that everyone has the same "monkey brain" and is easily distracted, and hiking helps to concentrate and focus on their minds. One day, I decided to hike to the Hollywood sign. I knew that I would spend about eight hours roundtrip because it was a long distance (about 10 miles) from my house. So I prepared everything before I left. I thought it would be challenging and would take a lot of effort. I started out around 8 a.m. and hiked about two hours to the Observatory. I really enjoyed seeing the beautiful scenery. Then I hiked further and felt excited and enjoyed it. The higher I went, the more stunning the views. Sometimes I meditated and it made me more relaxed, calm and balanced. Furthermore, the air was so fresh and pure so it was easy to practice forgiveness and let things go while I felt angry and fearful. I needed to see the Hollywood sign closer with my eyes. When I walked a long distance and many hours, I saw a lot of people walking with their families with the same goal as me. I also saw a lot of people that rode horses and people walking their dogs. Finally, I arrived at the Hollywood sign around noon. I was so excited that my mission was complete. I spent about one hour taking lots of pictures and enjoying amazing views before heading down. It was a really great memory. I saw a photographer who waited until the sunset to capture the red, yellow and orange sky as the sun met the Hollywood sign, just like a postcard. That day, I spent a lot of valuable time. I needed to overcome my obstacles and difficult situation by having a new experience. After that, every time when I walked up to the top of Hollywood Mountain, I felt happiness, forgiveness and joy.

Tutor – Julia Naman

Orienteering Is for Everyone
By Katerina B.

Some people have a natural awareness of their surroundings, they have a photographic memory, and know along with the four cardinal directions, their position in space. If you do not belong to these lucky humans, this story may be helpful to you.

Unfortunately, I could easily and in a blink of the eye get lost. Sometimes, finding my car in a parking lot or an exit at a big shopping center is a challenge. Once in the evening, I even witnessed how a young woman with a child and a bewildered look on her face was pacing between rows of cars looking for her car after their soccer game. She was on the verge of crying when I approached her to help. I felt sorry for her, but at the same time relieved that I was not the only one in need of GPS or a map with the mark "You are here."

Several years ago, my husband introduced our children and me to the sport of orienteering, his childhood interest. Orienteering is a sport involving the mind and body. You need to find every checkpoint on a course using a map and a compass. You learn to recognize the terrain, read the map, choose a better route, and even count your steps and watch your pace if you are advanced in orienteering. There are usually several courses offered at each competition that have different lengths and difficulty. Therefore, after becoming familiar with the shortest and easiest course, you may move on to more challenging and physically intensive ones.

Although you might know about orienteering as a part of scouting programs or military training, it is a well-known sport in the world. The first orienteering event held in North America was organized in 1941 at Dartmouth College in Hanover, New Hampshire, by an army officer, but regular events started in the 1960s. Orienteering USA, officially known as the United States Orienteering Federation (USOF), was founded in 1971. The Los Angeles Orienteering Club, which my family has joined, holds dozens of competitions every year in various locations like Mt. Pinos, Barton Flats, Santa Fe Dam, Vasquez Rocks, and so on.

From the very beginning, my family benefited from orienteering. We visited a lot of regional parks and national forests in Southern California and recognized many nice people passionate about orienteering. I am learning to notice more key objects on my way, and my confidence is growing with practice. My children's skills are progressing amazingly: my 9-year-old daughter is starting to run her courses independently, and my teenager son wins in his youth category. Orienteering encourages all of us to stay in a top physical form to the best of our abilities. My husband and son are competitive on advanced courses, so they need to practice reading maps while running because comprehending the course is more difficult with increasing speed and heart rate. Also, this sport affects me as a parent, it converts me from a constantly worrying mother to a calm and confident one. I am aware of my son's ability to create a full three-dimensional map in his mind with the mark "You are here," whether he is in a regional park or an urban area.

Orienteering is an affordable sport that suits any age group and fitness level. It does not need anything but a pair of comfortable training shoes, a compass, and an e-stick to punch the controls, but it gives you even more than you might wish. You will have plenty of busy weekends with family and friends in various places. You will never worry about having your workout done because even the recreational course gives you this opportunity. You will find a new passion in your life and maybe a new family to belong to. Enjoying nature, sharing similar interests with others, being excited about finding another checkpoint or sometimes the finish line are worthy reasons to start this never-ending adventure. Moving is life, and orienteering is the best way to stay active and alive! P.S. If you want to learn more about orienteering use this link: http://www.laorienteering.org

Tutor – Katherine Gifford

To Own the Moon
By Cindy Yanke

I wish I can own the moon.

I can make the moon be my world, my shepherd.

I would like to live in moonland, up high where no one is around.

– so peaceful – surrounded by millions of stars brightening the Earth.

I am in moonland.

I get to hug the moon.

Wherever the moon goes, I will go.

And I get to see the dark night moonland.

When the moon rises, all the darkness disappears and it lights the world – just light magic.

What is the moon made of?

Where does the light come from?

I would like to own the moon.

I get to find all the moon secrets,

Only singing of night brightening the whole world.

Just by itself, up high, then slowly going away to his planet.

He must be living in a beautiful land up in the sky.

His smiling big face lights up the dark night.

I will own the moon.

I will make the moon light up the world...

Tutor – Martha Kennedy

Collection of Poems
By E. I.

I Like Rain

Rain comes.

I wear a jacket, socks, and boots, and long pants.

I open my umbrella.

I walk in the rain.

I feel happy.

I like the rain.

Rainbows

Rainbows are red, yellow,

green, indigo, and violet.

I like rainbows.

Halloween

I turn off the light.

It is Halloween.

Children want candy.

Pies

I like apple pie,

Blueberry pie, pumpkin pie,

I like peach pie too.

My Christmas Tree

My tree has yellow lights.

The top is a star.

It has white ribbons.

It has ornaments too.

Two presents under the tree for me.

Tutor – Eileen Stephens

Oysters
By Sotheavy Chev

Rocky   Yummy

Floating   Slurping   Drooling

I love eating yummy oysters

Food

Tutor – Joan Wells

Unexpected Happenings

"I do not remember what happened next. My mother said that I was crossing the road when she saw me get run over by a group of donkeys."

Ninon Sauçeda, "One Summer Evening," p. 90

Guadaron Island
By Zaida Maytorena

I went to Mexico to visit my mother. When we arrived at my mother's house, she was happy. I asked for my brother Priciliano, but she told me that he was on Guadaron Island with his son and wife. I asked her when they would be sending him some groceries. She told me on Saturday his children Reyna and Omar and his son-in-law Luis would visit him and bring some. My mother said I could prepare to go. My daughter, Diana, and my niece Selene also prepared for the trip. I went to the store and bought meat to make carne asada there on the island.

The next day, we drove to the fishing port where Luis lived. Then we put all the groceries and five gallons of water into a small motor boat. We were so happy because we were going to the island. While Luis drove the boat slow and safe, we could see the mangrove trees and the birds. It was high tide. We soon arrived at the island. We took the groceries and we walked into the sand dunes to my brother's campsite. Pricito my brother's son saw us walking into the sand dunes, so he took his horse to help us with what we brought with us. After a hard walk in the sand, we arrived at the campsite. We were hungry and thirsty because we had walked 30 minutes.

Later, I cooked the meat that I had prepared for carne asada, and I made some quesadillas, which we enjoyed with Coca-Cola. We had a happy day with my brother's family. It was 5 p.m., time to come back to my mother's house. We returned to the place where we had left the boat and the tide was going out, so it was no longer in the water. We pulled the boat into the water and started our journey home.

Then Luis suggested digging for clams. I agreed because I thought that Luis knew the area. Then as he drove the boat around the island and the tide continued to go out, the boat stopped. The sun was almost down. My brother, who was on the island, heard the boat motor stop, but he didn't pay attention. My nephew wanted to call my sister-in-law Inelva on his phone and tell her that we were stuck in the sand because of the low tide. However, Pricito's cell battery died, so we didn't have communication with anybody.

Later the sun set and it started to get cold and windy. We were wearing life jackets, which protected us from the cold wind, but it was so cold that my teeth were chattering and my body was shaking. Also my tennis shoes were wet. Luis told us to get down between the benches of the boat to keep warm. I was worried because the wind was too cold. Finally, the tide came back and the boat floated again. Now, Luis started the motor and drove to the deepest water to get back to the fishing port. I felt afraid. It was a very dark night and it was hard to see. Luis needed to drive between the mangrove trees and he had trouble finding the floating markers showing the way. Finally he found the path, but we had little gas. At last, we arrived at the fishing port at 1 a.m. almost dead from cold weather. It was unsafe to drive in the middle of the night because of dangerous people on the road, but we needed to get to my mother's house. We arrived there at 2:00 a.m. It was a good trip, but next time we would pay attention to the tide.

Tutor – Lisa Zufferey

One Summer Evening
By Ninon Sauceda

I was born in Veracruz, Mexico. The first ten years of my life we were living in a little town called Boca del Rio. The town was close to the beach. It had a few roads made of dirt. My parents and grandparents lived in the same town. I have two sisters and two brothers. We all enjoyed living in Boca del Rio. During summer evenings, my mother sat out front of the house and talked with the neighbors. While she did that, I played with the neighborhood kids.

The evenings of summer in my hometown were very fun. The moms socialized. Everybody shared food and refreshments. They had conversations about everything, shared recipes, and ate at the same time. The kids had fun playing old games like hide and seek, jump rope, marbles, and many more games. The kids enjoyed eating food, snacks, cookies, and candies that their moms shared with everybody. These gatherings were very nice for the kids. Everybody participated. Kids did not have many toys like now. In those days, the kids didn't have technology. They could have fun, be outside, and experience nature.

I was five years old and, as usual, everybody was outside when suddenly we all heard an intense sound. We heard a sound like thunder. We all turned and looked. The people stopped and became silent and confused. All we could see was a cloud of dust. Everyone was stunned by what they saw. The panic took control. They all were terrified, and the kids started crying. The only thing they could see was dust. After a moment, some moms reacted and took their kids inside my home. The other moms stayed outside next to my mother.

I do not remember what happened next. My mother said that I was crossing the road when she saw me get run over by a group of donkeys. I was playing with the other kids, when I saw my friend Nena. Her house was on the other side of the road. I started crossing the road to go to her. There was a noise that sounded like stomping. My mother saw a group of donkeys running towards me. The donkeys used to pass by that road every evening. It was a group of a dozen donkeys. They were huge and strong, and normally calm. That evening they were wild.

As soon as they left, she saw a big cloud of dust. When all the dust faded away, she saw me on the ground, and came running toward me. The neighbors and the kids were afraid. I was unconscious.

She picked me up and took me inside the house. My mother told my dad what happened. My dad rushed to get the doctor. All the parents and kids were around my bed in my bedroom waiting for the doctor. Everybody was scared. Time passed very slowly. My mother said, "We are going to hold hands and we are going to pray."

My father came back with the doctor. Only my parents were permitted to be in the room during the time he had examined me. As soon as he finished checking on me, I woke up. I could not remember anything that had happened. There were only a few bruises on my legs, but "luckily no broken bones," the doctor said to my parents. The other mothers heard that I had woken up and they approached the room where I was with my parents. Everybody was happy to see that I was ok. My mother said to me, "You are a miracle." She explained to me what had happened. After this event, we all continued to enjoy summer evenings in my hometown. I learned from this experience to be careful when I am crossing any road and ask for my mother's permission.

Tutor – Corina Lopez

No Longer A Home
By Elen Alsabea

We all believe that our homes are places of safety, tranquility, and warmth.

A home is like your mother's bosom to which you turn when you feel afraid. A home is not just a roof and walls. It is more than this. Home can make you feel like a fetus feels in its mother's womb. Can you imagine how hard it is to change your belief about home giving a peaceful feeling?

I used to think my home was my refuge and place of safety until I saw the breaking news on TV broadcasting the devastating earthquake in Syria. I saw homes fall on their own people, not caring about the victims being babies, elderly, sick, healthy, poor, or rich. I couldn't call those buildings homes any more.

They are just stone houses.

My Syrian people have struggled with civil war for over 12 years. In one moment they forgot the pain of those 12 bitter years. That pain was diminished by the shock of the earthquake. At that time I didn't see the news report as news. I saw it as a life-changing disaster that befell my Syrian family.

At that moment I felt I had millions of brothers and sisters in danger. That earthquake shook the earth in Syria and shook my heart with grief. As I was thousands of miles away on the other side of the world, my spatial distance from my homeland made me feel heartbroken and helpless at not being able to give support.

Forgive me my Syrian family, because I was not with you to remove the rubble from your broken bodies or give a sip of water to your thirsty lips. If I cannot embrace you with my arms I will embrace you with my heart, my sisters and brothers.

Tutor – Trudy Waldron

Retreat

By Wensung Hsu

In 1949, Chiang Kai-Shek, the leader of the Republic of China retreated from mainland China to Taiwan. There have been two Chinese governments from that time till now. I believe this is the most important historical event from the last 100 years for all the Chinese.

After World War II, China ended an eight-year fight with Japan, but the Civil War started. Mao Zedong's power was getting bigger, it forced the government under Chiang Kai-Shek and the military to retreat to Taiwan. On October 10, 1949, Mao established a Communist government called the People's Republic of China.

My father at that time was in the army. He needed to follow the army retreat to Taiwan. My mother was the only one he could take with him, other family members stayed on mainland China in their hometown. I was born in 1951, then my sister and brother joined the family. The five of us lived in Taiwan. In this new place we had no relatives around. My parents never saw their parents again. We children only heard stories about our grandparents, uncles, and aunts. Someone stole my parents' suitcase during the retreat. They lost all the family pictures and wedding pictures. I feel sad for not knowing my grandparents and even more for not knowing what they looked like.

This event caused a lot of suffering and tragedy for the Chinese. Even now the two governments still are against each other. This event is not only important in history, it affects life today and the future too!

Tutor – Kathleen Cejka

The Accident
By Joy Phillips

On Sunday, February 12, 2023, my husband and I wanted to go out to celebrate Valentine's Day early. We wanted to go to the Outback Steakhouse restaurant, but we got into an accident before we got there.

I was driving on Ford Street, toward Redlands Boulevard, and another driver was coming in the opposite direction. The driver wanted to turn left onto the on-ramp for Interstate 10. We both had the green light, but I had the right of way.

We both got out of our cars after the collision. The other car's driver was a woman. She came to my car and apologized to me and to my husband. My husband was the passenger in our car. The other car's passenger was her teenage son. Thank God nobody was hurt.

It was lucky that the other driver had automotive insurance. Police, fire, and EMT officers came. The fire and EMT responders left after we told them that no one was hurt. The police officer took pictures of our driver's licenses and our insurance policies. The police officer had me take a picture of the damage to our car and the license plate of the other car. I asked the police officer for his name and the accident's case number.

When my husband and I got home, my husband tried to report the accident online, but he was unsuccessful. The next morning he was able to talk with a representative from the insurance company. He gave her the information about the accident. She gave us the adjuster's name that would handle our case.

I was still able to drive my car. I took it to a collision shop for a damage estimate on February 16. It took the collision shop about a month to have the estimate for the insurance company.

On March 15, I took the car back to the collision shop for repair. The guy at the shop said that it might be finished in two weeks.

Now, on April 5, my car is still in the shop. The guy said that he is waiting for a part.

Waiting for the part to arrive was stressful. The repair work was completed on May 10, and the next day I picked up my car.

The accident was not a good thing for everyone involved. There are a lot of matters to deal with. From now on, I told myself, I have to drive more defensively.

Tutor – Toni Curley

Everyday Issues at Work: Part 2
By C. Pineda

New year, but at work everything is the same. Today, I am training a new employee. First I helped him put together his cart, then later I saw him coming inside the janitor's closet. "Are you on break?" I said. "No," he answered, "I just don't have any empty rooms to clean." I explained to him that even if he doesn't have any empty rooms to clean, he needs to clean every room. He asked me to show him what he needed to do. So I went with him and tried to show him how to clean a room when suddenly he said, "I will be back, is that okay?" I said, "Okay."

By the time he came back, I had already finished cleaning the room. He told me that he was sorry but he needed time for himself. By that time, it was almost lunchtime and I didn't have my cart ready, so I went to look for supplies. I went inside the janitor's closet and took a bucket from the cart that was inside (I had given my bucket to the new employee). On the way back to my work area, my mind was telling me I was doing something wrong because every day we complain about missing work equipment from our cart, and that was exactly what I was doing.

On another occasion, I wanted to tell one of the supervisors something, so I called her attention and said to her, "You guys are doubling us too much. Did you know that some of the rooms haven't been cleaned for 5 days?" I explained to her that on Thursday, which is my last day of work, I can only finish cleaning one side of the unit. So on Friday and Saturday, my partner cannot do much because she is working by herself. Then on Sunday, when I go back to my regular schedule, I can't do much either because I'm working on both sides. So she replied, "Who is your partner?" And I answered, "That doesn't really matter who my partner is." I felt bad for the patient, they looked like a little animal inside a fence. That room looked so dirty and we ended the conversation.

Aside from talking about my coworkers, sometimes when the nurses are taking care of the patients, they miss the trash can and it goes to the floor. One time, I had just finished cleaning a discharge room when they moved another patient into that room. They took the IV posts from the clean room and put it back in the dirty room where the patient came from. So I had to clean it again. But I love what I do. I even don't care if they don't tell me when they have a spill, smear everything on the floors with their shoes and track it to the other rooms, make the floor very sticky, and then let me know after.

Another time at work, I fell in a patient's room that I was cleaning. I stepped back and tripped on a wheel of a couch and fell back against the patient's bed. I tried to get up really quickly, telling her that I was really sorry, but I could not stop laughing. I think that I scared her, she was asking if I was okay. I told her that I was okay, then I felt so sorry, like she needed that on top of being there in a hospital. But I could not stop laughing. Outside of the room was a nurse assistant, but she thought that I was moving the furniture in the room to clean the back side.

Every day we have to deal with things like this because some people have their minds set and work smart, not hard. I've been asking myself: if you are leaving your work for the next worker or the next shift, you don't care about your job, or maybe you care so much that you just leave it for the next shift person in order to be done right because you don't know how to do it the right way.

Tutor – Nancy Luong

Reading Reflections

"Your unique story of standing up for girls' rights has been reaching and inspiring the world."

Cinderella Tran, "Malala," p. 102

Reading Reflections

The Redlands Adult Literacy Program encourages learners to read books as an integral part of their literacy journey. Literacy teams may select a book from the library's adult literacy collection or other sources, guided by learner interest or by one of the program's book clubs. Biannually, the adult literacy community selects a book and invites the Redlands community to participate in reading events that celebrate the gift of literacy.

In 2022, the adult literacy program celebrated reading by exploring the story <u>Malala – My Story of Standing Up for Girls Rights</u> by Malala Yousafzai. This autobiographical book was chosen, in part, because Malala Yousafzai represents the courage of learners who seek improved literacy despite the challenges they may face. This section includes the reactions of two adult learners who were inspired to write about Malala's story.

Other adult learners wrote about other books they had read. One adult learner wrote about <u>Still Alice</u> by Lisa Genova. This novel about someone suffering from Alzheimer's disease increased the learner's awareness about the impact of Alzheimer's on the individual, their families, and the community. The classic book, <u>Anne of Green Gables</u> by Lucy Maud Montgomery inspired another adult learner to write. <u>Anne of Green Gables</u> has been a perennial favorite of the adult literacy program and it is a joy to celebrate its classic themes with the literacy community.

To foster reading comprehension and vocabulary building, the Redlands Adult Literacy Program has two book clubs: one that meets on Monday mornings, and a learner-led book club that meets monthly. Below is a list of some of the books that the book clubs read this year. We invite you to consider adding them to your reading list!

Recommended Books

Jonathan Livingston Seagull by Richard Bach

From Scratch by Gail Anderson

The Miraculous Journey of Edward Tulane by Kate DiCamillo

Queen Serene by Greta Gorsuch

The Spy by Suzanne Kamata

Doors to the Sky by Tana Reiff

Island of the Blue Dolphins by Scott O'Dell

A Horse Called Courage by Anne Schraff

What Was Ellis Island? by Patricia Brennan Demuth

Borders by Thomas King

Malala
By Cinderella Tran

I always read books about famous old people to learn something from them.

Finally, I chose your book to read. Amazingly, you were only a normal child like others, yet you became the most famous Nobel Peace Prize-winning girl in history.

Your love and your dream came true, but your mission did not allow you to stop here.

On CNN, I watched the news that Airbnb co-founder Mr. Joe Gebbia donated 25 million dollars to The Malala Fund. That was huge money.

I know your long-term journey is to help the youth go to school and finish college in your country and in neighboring countries, too.

Your unique story of standing up for girls' rights has been reaching and inspiring the world.

God saved you because He received your letter asking for the strength and courage to make the world a better place. You did it, Malala!

Tutor – Kim Green

Malala

By Alexandra Suárez, Runner-up, Writer-to-Writer Challenge

Dear Malala,

While I was reading your book I was immersed in your life. Thank you for letting me be part of your story. The way you wrote your book taught me not only about a culture but also about your beliefs, your faith. I could see your personal relationship with God (with Allah) in all your expressions. In every word you wrote I saw how much you care about people, for their present and their future. I could understand the commitment you have with your life's purpose. You put aside your fears, your own struggles in order to pursue your dreams. You found the strength to encourage those who lose their desire to fight along the way. Above all, your attitude of thankfulness to God throughout your journey was the seed to what you achieved.

Your book has inspired me to be courageous in any circumstance. I learned from you that we always have the opportunity to read the episodes (events) of our lives with a constructive view. The maturity you showed in your book, by accepting the good and the bad in your life, is a model for every woman, every girl, every person . The love you had for your parents, for your family, made me realize how important it is to grow up in an environment full of love. You made me think about 1 Corinthians 13 "...but if I do not have love, I am nothing." You walked step by step with the love God gave you.

In summarizing your words I started to think about the reason I'm here, at this moment, in this city, in this life. I have been thinking about what kind of love I give while I'm serving others. Now I'm asking myself if I am living the way God had planned for me? I started wondering if I've had an impact in someone's life and if I did, was it positive? I want to live as you have, thinking about giving my best in every step, in every choice, as if it is my last day in this world. Thank you for opening my eyes with love.

Sincerely,

Alexandra Suárez

Tutor – Barbara Vester

The Unknown Life of an Alzheimer's Patient
By Katerina B.

How much can you know about Alzheimer's if you have not experienced this misfortune with your family or friends? Everyone who will read the fictional, but truthful book "Still Alice" by Lisa Genova will remember its touching and sorrowful narration about Dr. Alice Howland. *USA Today* described the book as "A poignant portrait of Alzheimer's...Not a book you will forget about." What made this story so engrossing and unforgettable?

Before I opened this book I knew almost nothing about Alzheimer's. As far as I was aware, none of my ancestors was diagnosed with Alzheimer's, but truth be told most of them either passed away in their sixties or were not examined by doctors looking for brain issues. I thought that Alzheimer's was quite a rare problem that affected only elderly people in their mid-seventies or older, but this story introduced me to information that ten percent of people with Alzheimer's are under sixty-five years old, and some of them are in their fifties. The only point I was not mistaken about was the cruelty and severity of Alzheimer's toward its victims.

In the book, Dr. Alice Howland was a psychology professor at Harvard University for twenty-five years and lectured all over the world. At the age of fifty she was diagnosed with early-onset Alzheimer's disease. First, Alice could not recall an accurate word during her speech at a conference. Then, she totally forgot about her flight to a different city. Finally, Alice got lost while she was running on a familiar route. Boom! She could no longer feel safe and normal, she did not know if she could rely on herself or not.

She wished she had cancer instead because she would have a chance to fight it. Her family and friends would "rally behind her battle and consider it noble." Instead, Alzheimer's patients were treated like they were insane and became outcasts in the society because they looked physically healthy, while their brains were self-destructing.

Alice's deterioration was obvious to her, so she felt miserable and lonely. She could no longer follow the thread of a conversation, the plot of a book, or a movie. She could not enjoy communicating, reading, or watching TV because it made her keenly aware of how lost she was. However, Alice did not give up. She needed a new society to belong to, so she started to look for a support group for Alzheimer's patients, and found nothing. It seemed that people cared more about caregivers than patients. Alice organized her own support group for people with Alzheimer's and dementia. More than a year after being diagnosed, she gave an influential presentation to the annual Dementia Care Conference where she encouraged professionals to make earlier diagnoses, and asked caregivers to empower, not to limit those with Alzheimer's. She said, "I am not someone dying. I am someone living with Alzheimer's." At that moment, I was crying. I did not realize that Alzheimer's could destroy someone's personality so fast. Alzheimer's patients do not have a chance to live with their families for a long time. They cannot close their days with dignity and with a recognition of a loved one whose hand they would hold in the last moment.

This year and a half, which was lived with Dr. Alice Howland, made me aware of the life circumstances of every Alzheimer's patient. I feel deeply sorry for them not only while I am driving by the Alzheimer's Special Care Center with its neat and quiet campus. Now, I can imagine the routine behind its fences and the patients who may have had interesting social and satisfying personal lives and who are able to have just the predetermined, withdrawn lives, which may be full of sorrow and pain. This book teaches you compassion for others, and inspires you to love yourself and your life. You need to spend your future years with purpose because being healthy and physically independent, being who you are, should not be taken for granted, but as a fortunate gift.

Tutor – Katherine Gifford

Dear Ms. Marsden
By Yesenia JV

Dear Ms. Marden,

I read your book, <u>Anne of Green Gables</u>, at the Library Book Club. I like the character Anne because she is so brave. She had many troubles in her life. She knows how to resolve her problems. I also like the character Matthew because he was so kind to Anne.

There are many parts of the story that I liked. I like that when they go to school, they put their milk in the little river, they did not have a refrigerator. I like the part when Diana and Anne were having a tea party. It was Anne's first tea party and they were very happy. They were having fun and didn't know they got the wrong bottle and were drinking alcohol! Diana got drunk and Diana's mother was very mad that she got drunk. She said that Anne isn't a good friend for Diana. Anne apologized to Diana's mother. Another part that I liked was when Anne made the cake for the minister and his wife. She thought she used vanilla and it was liniment for Marilla's headache. Anne thought the cake was going to be good. She watched the faces for their reaction. It didn't taste good and Anne was disappointed. I also like the part with Gilbert. Gilbert liked Anne, but she did not like him. I think she really did like him and didn't want to say it. They became friends at the end of the story.

This book reminded me of where I grew up. I grew up on a ranch in Jalisco, Mexico. Anne and I both grew up with horses on the ranch. We were the same because the town was far from our houses. We both walked to school. My house did not have electricity and we illuminated the rooms with oil lamps. Anne lights up her house with oil lamps too. We both used firewood to cook. There were some things that were different from me and Anne. Snow doesn't fall on my ranch and my life was not as difficult as Anne's. She suffered a lot in the orphanage.

Thank you again for writing this book about Anne of Green Gables. I felt comfortable reading the book and I really liked it. I wanted to continue reading the book to see what happened to Anne and Gilbert.

Sincerely,

Yesenia

Tutor – Joan Prehoda

Family Literacy

The Family Literacy Program recognizes that parents are their children's first and most important teachers. The program introduces families to the value and pleasure of reading and writing together. The writings in this chapter reflect interactive activities shared during family literacy meetings.

Dad

By Angela and Elian

Dad

Involved   Lovely

Working   Talking   Crying

Cries with sad movies

Colleague

Family Literacy – April 2023

Daddy
By Mia Gadea

Daddy

Handsome   Loyal

Building   Eating   Snoring

Daddy is a wonderful father

Man

Family Literacy – April 2023

The Day We Became Friends
By Matthew Li

It was just a natural August afternoon at Cope Middle School. Our class was just playing a game of Head-up 7-Up. When I chose the right person and chose a thumb, I, for some reason, stared at the person that I chose. He stared back at me and immediately chose me to be his friend.

After that day, we started talking to each other. It was the weirdest way to make a friend, but that is how we became friends. I made friends with his friends and now we are like very good friends.

We joined our school's sports intramural soccer game with all our friends. I hope we still have the same classes next year!

Family Literacy – February 2023

Luisa
By Lu

Luisa

Smart   Beautiful

Dancing   Reading   Drawing

Brave on every step

Girl

Brother
By Lu

Brother

Funny   Sportman

Hopping   Caring   Friendly

Full of our love

Tomas

Family Literacy – April 2023

Carla
By Sandra Lahhoud

Carla

Cute Little

Laughing Crying Sleeping

Sleeping during sucking milk

Baby cousin

Family Literacy – April 2023

Soccer

By Edgar Munoz

Soccer

Happy   Sweaty

Kicking   Spinning   Catching

Enjoy it with friends

Game

Family Literacy – April 2023

Soccer Ball
Aydan

Soccer Ball

Black & White   Round

Kicking   Running   Rolling

I have many soccer balls

Ball

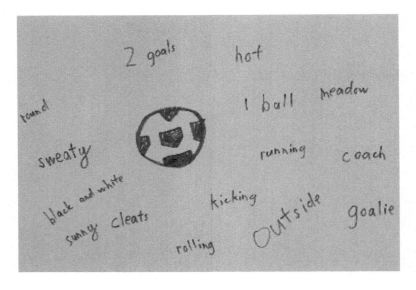

Family Literacy – April 2023

Parakeets

By Yaretzi Jimenez

Parakeets

Annoying   Big

Talking   Walking   Whistling

Like to stretch wings

Birds

Family Literacy – April 2023

Coco
By Jiarui

Coco

Cute   Fluffy

Eating   Sleeping   Cuddling

Like a Teddy Bear

Coki

Family Literacy – April 2023

Cat

By Joan Prehoda – Tutor
Yesenia and Yaretzi Jimenez Vidrio

Cat

Fluffy   Destructive

Jumping   Annoying   Running

He is handsome

Sebastian

Family Literacy – April 2023

Index of Authors

Acevedo, Norma—My Trials of Learning English 25
Allen, Frank—My Tutoring Story 52
Alsabea, Elen—Gratitude at Dawn 68
Alsabea, Elen—No Longer A Home 92
Angela and Elian—Dad 110
Aydan—Soccer Ball 116
B., Alec—My Life 51
B., Katerina—Orienteering Is for Everyone 81
B., Katerina—The Unknown Life of an Alzheimer's Patient 104
Ballesteros, Manuela—A Wonderful Family 69
Ballesteros, Manuela—Walking in the Hills 78
Becerra, Raul—Follow Your Dreams 47
Cannady, Darcel and Briseiry Roque—Our New Language 70
Castañeda, Armando—Pepito Caballero Castañeda Roque 56
Chev, Sotheavy—I Did My Best 50
Chev, Sotheavy—My Family Tree Memories 64
Chev, Sotheavy—Oysters 86
Corrin, Mark—On a Sunny Day 73
Corrin, Mark—The Trinity Church 31
Cruz, Peter—My Love for Photography 49
Dominguez, Rebeca—Talking with my Grandfather 62
E.I.—Collection of 'Mom' Poems 18
E.I.—Collection of Poems 84
Gadea, Mia—Daddy 111
Goff, Phillip—Me Myself I 55
Gutierrez, Mila—Life in Two Countries 28

Hsu, Wensung—Retreat	93
Jiarui—Coco	118
Jimenez, Yaretzi—Parakeets	117
Jimenez Vidrio, Yesenia and Yaretzi and Joan Prehoda—Cat	119
JV, Yesenia—Burritos with Salt	41
JV, Yesenia—Dear Ms. Marsden	106
K.K.—School in Punjab	37
Lahhoud, Sandra—Carla	114
Le, Rossy – My Dogs	66
Li, Matthew—The Day We Became Friends	112
Lu—Brother	113
Lu—Luisa	113
Marquez, Salma R. —My Life on a Ranch	36
Maytorena, Zaida—Guadaron Island	88
Munoz, Edgar—Soccer	115
Munoz, Paola—Going Back To My Country After 11 Years	34
Nyirady, Kwanlar—My New Home	30
Oake, Serena—Mom	24
Pacheco, Yanetzy—The Birth of My First Child	63
Pacheco, Yanetzy—The Birth of My Second Child	63
Phillips, Joy—The Accident	94
Pineda, C.—Everyday Issues at Work Part 2	96
Pineda, C.—When I Was Growing Up	38
Roque, Briseiry —Thank You!	16
Ryan, Mina—The Good Samaritan	14
Sauceda, Ninon —Dylan Rescued a Dog	22
Sauceda, Ninon—One Summer Evening	90

Sienglai, Apichat — Fire That Changed My Life 20

Sienglai, Apichat — Hike to Hollywood Sign 79

Suárez, Alexandra—Light at the End of the Tunnel? 32

Suárez, Alexandra – Malala 103

Tran, Cinderella – Malala 102

Velázquez, Emma – My Wonderful Short Visit to
    La Paz, Baja California 76

Vidrio, Ma, Isabel – My Diamante Poem 54

Vidrio, Ma, Isabel – Singing 40

Yanke, Cindy – My Daughter 15

Yanke, Cindy – To Own the Moon 83

Yanke, Cindy – Wisconsin 42

Zhou, Yanhong—My Tutor Helene 12

Our Services

Adult Literacy

The core of the Redlands Adult Literacy Program is one-to-one tutoring. An adult learner requests help with reading and writing, is assessed by the literacy coordinator, and then paired with a trained volunteer tutor. The tutor-learner team meets weekly for 1 1/2 hours for a minimum of 6 months. The tutor and learner work together on learner–identified reading and writing goals. All materials are provided without cost to the learner or tutor. Common learner goals include: reading a book, writing a letter, applying for employment, helping children with homework, and/or advancing their own education.

Family Literacy

The Family Literacy Program supports parents, grandparents, or guardians who are enrolled in the Adult Literacy Program and their children ages 13 or younger. The Family Literacy Program teaches strategies to families that encourage reading in the home, develop deeper communication between family members, and demonstrate the value of education. At each meeting, families receive books to build home libraries. Participation in the program helps family members work toward their personal learning goals.

Computer Literacy

To support adult learners' digital literacy goals, small group computer classes are available. At the beginning level, learners are taught how to use a mouse and keyboard, how to search the internet, and how to write a letter using Microsoft Word. Each learner creates a Gmail account and practices sending and receiving emails. Intermediate level computer courses reinforce and advance this learning and focus on literacy skills such as writing paragraphs or stories. Digital literacy skills are important for learners who have goals of obtaining employment, communicating with family, friends and/or teachers online, and competently using the internet in their daily lives.

Volunteer Support

Tutors attend tutor orientation and tutor training meetings to learn about the Redlands Adult Literacy Program and to practice using adult literacy materials. All tutors are invited to attend quarterly roundtable meetings and literacy workshops for continuing education, to discuss tutoring challenges, and to share ideas, tips, and tools that work. Volunteers also support the computer classes, fundraising efforts, and public outreach.

To Contact Us:

The Redlands Adult Literacy Program relies on its volunteers. If you are interested in learning more about becoming an adult literacy tutor or volunteer, please contact the Adult Literacy Coordinator at A.K. Smiley Public Library.

If you know of people who need help with reading and writing, encourage them to take the first step in changing their lives by contacting the Redlands Adult Literacy Program.

Diane Shimota, Adult Literacy Coordinator
Email: literacy@akspl.org
Phone: (909) 798-7565 x 4138
Visit the Adult Literacy webpage: www.akspl.org/literacy
Follow us on Instagram: *friendsofsmileylibrary*
Facebook: *Friends of A.K. Smiley Public Library*

A.K. Smiley Public Library
125 W. Vine Street
Redlands, CA 92373
(909) 798-7565
literacy@akspl.org

Literacy Changes Lives!

Support Adult Literacy

- Spread the word that literacy help is available at A.K. Smiley Public Library—most learners find out about the program from family and friends.
- Become a literacy volunteer.
- Donate to the Redlands Adult Literacy Program.
- Come to literacy events.
- Join the Friends of A.K. Smiley Public Library and purchase books at the Friends Bookstore.

Available for check-out at A.K. Smiley Public Library.

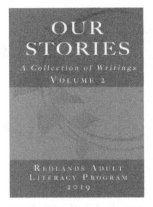
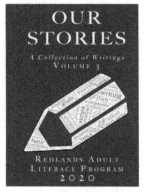

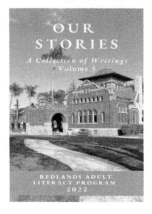
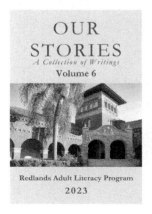

Made in the USA
Middletown, DE
09 September 2023